THE VICTORIA AND ALBERT COLOUR BOOKS

FIRST PUBLISHED IN GREAT BRITAIN BY
WEBB & BOWER (PUBLISHERS) LIMITED
9 COLLETON CRESCENT, EXETER, DEVON EX2 4BY
IN ASSOCIATION WITH THE VICTORIA AND ALBERT MUSEUM, LONDON

COPYRIGHT © WEBB & BOWER (PUBLISHERS) LIMITED,
THE TRUSTEES OF THE VICTORIA AND ALBERT MUSEUM,
COOPER THIRKELL LIMITED 1985

BOOK, COVER AND SLIP CASE DESIGN BY COOPER THIRKELL LIMITED

PRODUCTION BY NICK FACER

TYPESET IN GREAT BRITAIN BY THE VANTAGE GROUP

PRINTED AND BOUND IN HONG KONG BY
MANDARIN OFFSET INTERNATIONAL LIMITED

BRITISH LIBRARY CATALOGUING IN PUBLICATION DATA

ORNATE WALLPAPERS—(THE VICTORIA & ALBERT COLOUR BOOKS; 4)
1. WALLPAPER
1. SAUNDERS, GILL II SERIES
747'.3 NK3395

ISBN 0-86350-087-0

THE VICTORIA AND ALBERT COLOUR BOOKS

ORNATE
WALLPAPERS

WEBB & BOWER

MCMLXXXV

 THE WALLPAPER samples illustrated in this volume are taken from three pattern books in the Department of Prints & Drawings at the Victoria & Albert Museum. They are almost certainly from the firm which was later known as Jeffrey & Co. and contain in all 900 specimens of wallpapers, borders and corner-pieces, each inscribed with titles and other notes. The papers, arranged chronologically, are dated 1837 to 1852. Over this period extensive mechanisation revolutionised production in the wallpaper industry and machine processes largely replaced hand-printing with wood-blocks.

From about 1806 continuous rolls of paper were available, where previously a 'piece' (11½ yards) had been made up of several sheets joined. In 1816 Edward Cooper invented a machine which could print from curved stereotyped plates, but the process was not used for wallpaper printing until 1830 when the Excise authorities finally lifted their embargo. In 1835 came Thomas Greig's machine for colour printing and embossing from three separate metal cylinders in register, followed in 1839 by Joseph Birche's process of drying rapidly-printed paper. In the same year the Potters of Darwen, Lancashire, patented a power-driven roller printer adapted from calico-printing machinery. The limitation of this process was the frequency of the repeat, but it made possible the mass production of cheap papers. According to an 1853 publication, *Novelties, Inventions and Curiosities in Arts & Manufacture* the cylinder-printing methods produced wallpapers at a cost of a farthing per yard.

By the mid-nineteenth century wallpaper was to be found in almost every household; a fashionable and now affordable decorative accessory. Papers were shown in exhibitions of art and industry including the Great Exhibition of 1851. Here papers reproducing Old Master paintings and a 24-foot frieze depicting the Elgin marbles in *trompe l'oeil* (by Jeffrey, Allen & Co.) revealed the extent to which technical achievements had outstripped standards of design. As early as 1839 the Art Union had warned, in relation to the competition from French manufacturers, that through 'the non-employment of artistic skill on our part we find ourselves considerably in the background. Machinery will not do all'. Florid naturalism and pictorial designs were especially deplored by those intent on improving standards of design. The architect A.W.N. Pugin and the designer Owen Jones both advocated flat two-dimensional patterns, and devised their own wallpapers to demonstrate their theories. Jones was later to work for Jeffrey & Co. Under the management of Metford Warner from 1866 the company became one of the most innovative and influential wallpaper manufacturers of the nineteenth century. By an imaginative

policy of commissioning artists and architects, including E.W. Godwin, William Burges and Walter Crane, they raised standards of design throughout the industry.

The samples in these early pattern books, represent the vast range of styles and patterns which flooded onto the market with the advent of mechanisation and mass production. A number of them are relatively simple designs with an obvious repeat such as trellis, spot or diaper patterns. More ambitious are the pictorial papers; one attractive example features Tintern Abbey (1838) and is a fine example of the Gothic taste which was much in evidence throughout this period. The style was vigorously promoted by Pugin, the architect and decorator of the Houses of Parliament, though he deplored its haphazard application to contemporary wallpaper design.

Nevertheless the popularity of the style is evident in the number of 'Gothic' papers imitating stonework and plaster mouldings which are included here.

Wallpaper has always been an imitative medium, used as an inexpensive substitute for other wallcoverings such as embossed leather, tapestry, brocade and chintz. In the nineteenth century flock papers imitating velvets and brocades, and floral papers imitating chintzes were particularly popular. Flocking had been an established technique since the fifteenth century: a design was stencilled in adhesive on a coloured ground and then powdered shearings of wool were scattered over the surface. The result was a rich velvety relief. One of the papers included here is a reproduction of an historic design, the magnificent flock paper hung in the Whitehall Offices of the Privy Council in the 1730's. The original copied a contemporary Genoese silk damask. The design was in continual demand for grander houses and for State apartments and it is still available today. Chintz had been in use as a wallcovering since the seventeenth century: in 1663 Samuel Pepys bought his wife a 'Chinkse, that is, a paynted Indian Callico for to line her new study, which is very pretty'. Papers copying chintz patterns were soon introduced but eventually 'chinz' came to mean any floral pattern.

William Morris, though he championed craft methods against industrial processes, accepted as inevitable the machine printing of wallpapers and advised other designers accordingly: 'I think the real way to deal successfully with designing for paper hangings is to accept their mechanical nature frankly, to avoid falling into the trap of trying to make your paper look as if it were painted by hand. Here is the place, if anywhere, for dots and lines and hatchings; mechanical enrichment is of the first necessity in it'.

By accepting the limitations of the process the best machine-printed papers were subtle and restrained, in contrast to the excess which marked so much Victorian design. Those cylinder-printed papers of the late 1830's such as 'King Star' (1839) with its *irisé* (blended colour) background certainly bear this out.

THE PLATES

Paisley Stripe
2 prints
Rack 230

Chintz Spray
2 prints
Rack 176

Taffeta
Chintz
3 prints
Rack 217

Berry Chintz

Rose Stripe

Geranium Chintz

4

1851

Last Trellis
1—172

Coral Spring
1—173

The Tulip
1—265

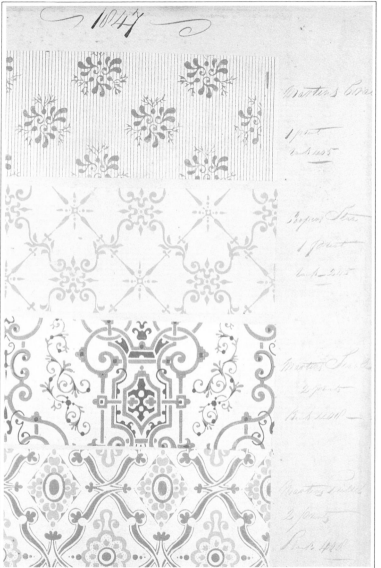

1847

Fin Rosette

Comet

Irons Vandyke 2 prints B.h 232

January 1841

Rose Cylinder

Walker's Daisy Trellis

Maltese Damask

9

No. 38 marlo

No. 6 marlo

No. 34 marlo

No. 32 marlo

Destroyed
1876

II

Doris Griffin   3 — 264

Harkins Star   2 — 408

Marone Stripe   2 — 261

Destroyed
1876

Eton Filling   2 — 263

2/ Prints Rack
Hay Edge

4 Prints
Prints
Rack 55

Rack 53
Frieze
4 Prints

6 Prints
Rack 84

5 Prints
Rack 87

6 Prints
Rack

4 Prints
Rack 87

6 Prints
Rack 88

3 Prints
Rack 89

Syrian Damask 2 prints Rack 381

Octagon Star
2 Prints
Rack 245

Voyez's Star
2 Prints
Rack 313

Landers Marble
2 Cylinder
Rollers

Bead Panel
2 Prints
Rack 351

Norman Filling
1 Print
Rack 230

Victoria Flux
1 Print
Rack 3

Brathett filling
2 Prints
Rack 84

Spear filling
2 Prints
Rack 84

January — 1848

1852.

Hatch Stripe
1 — 281

Ring Filling
2 — 40

Grass
1 — 137

Chelsea Filling
1 — 82

1846.

Noels Convolvous
One print
Rack 245

Coopers Star
One print
Rack 245

Lee's Pin
2 prints
Rack 245

Bar Filling
One print
Rack 244

1849

Saxon Filling
1 – 410

281
Hants Hope

27

Shamrock
Filling
2 - 301

Voysey's Panel
5 - 45

Coventry Stripe
3 - 155

Lily ...
2 - 43

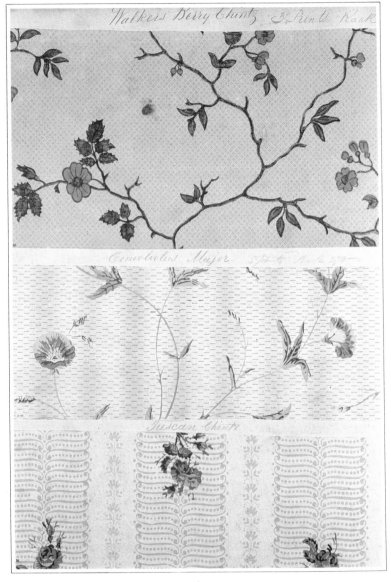

Walkers Berry Chintz. 3 Prints Rack

Convolvulus Major. 5 Prints No. 6 279

Tuscan Chintz

Ivy Trellis

3—99

3 Prints
Rack 44⅔
No 11

5 Prints
Rack =
54 4443

5 Prints
Rack 44.

French Anemone

Wild Pea 332

Gothic Pannel 2 ptents 360 Bush

33

4 Prints
Rack 443

Rack 446
5 Prints

5 Prints
Rack
448

35

Honeysuckle
2 — 122

Dog Rose
2 — 122

Convolvulus Major
2 — 122

Babway Chintz

85

3 Prints
Rack 313

Lilac Chintz

Rack
272
4 prints

Geranium Chintz

3 Prints
Rack 24.

Primrose Chintz

4 Prints
Rack
285

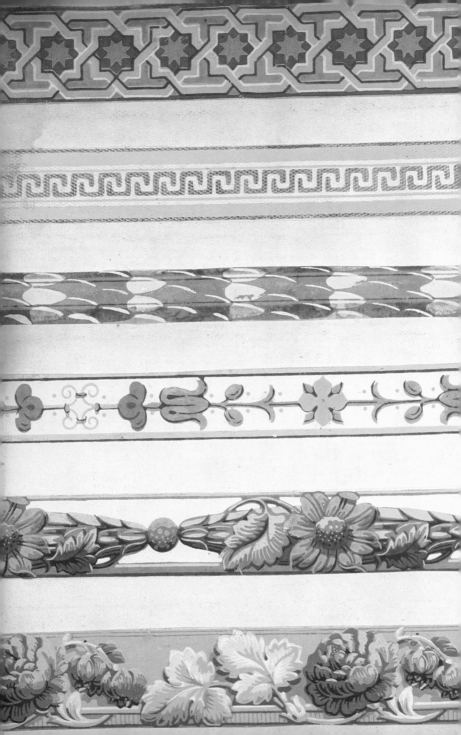